SCRIPTURE MASTERY
COLORING BOOK
THE BOOK OF MORMON

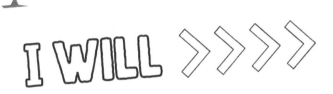

I WILL >>>>

GO & DO

THE THINGS THE **LORD** HATH COMMANDED

1 NEPHI 3:7

This book belongs to:

_____

About this Coloring Book

This coloring book includes the 25 Book of Mormon Scripture Mastery verses listed below. Enjoy coloring each passage as you memorize the words. On the back of each coloring page, fill-in-the-blank for each scripture passage.

1 Nephi 3:7	Alma 7:11—13
2 Nephi 2:25	Alma 32:21
2 Nephi 2:27	Alma 37:35
2 Nephi 9:28—29	Alma 39:9
2 Nephi 25:23, 26	Alma 41:10
2 Nephi 28:7—9	Helaman 5:12
2 Nephi 31:19—20	3 Nephi 12:48
2 Nephi 32:3	3 Nephi 18:15, 20—21
2 Nephi 32:8—9	Ether 12:6
Mosiah 2:17	Ether 12:27
Mosiah 3:19	Moroni 7:41
Mosiah 4:30	Moroni 7:45, 47—48
	Moroni 10:4—5

I WILL >>>>> GO & DO

THE THINGS THE LORD HATH COMMANDED

1 NEPHI 3:7

And it came to _____that
I, _____, said unto my
_____: I will go and do
the things which the
_____hath commanded,
for I _____that the Lord
_____no
commandments unto the
_____of men, save
he shall _____a way
for them that they may
_____the
thing which he
commandeth _____.

1 Nephi 3:7

Adam fell that men might be: and men are, that they might have

2 Nephi 2:25

_____fell that men might ___; and ____are, that they might have _____.

2 Nephi 2:25

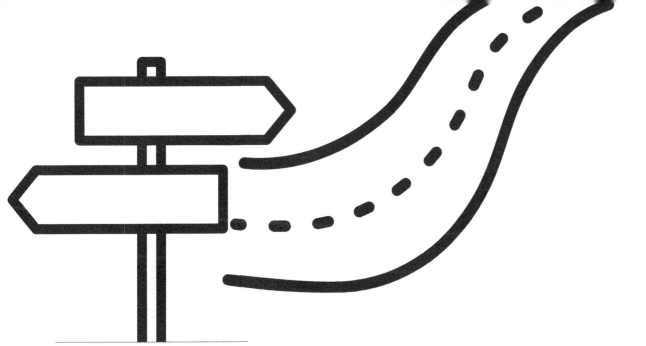

WHEREFORE, MEN ARE FREE...TO CHOOSE LIBERTY AND ETERNAL LIFE...OR CAPTIVITY AND DEATH

2 NEPHI 2:27

Wherefore, _____are _____according to the flesh; and all _____are given them which are _____unto man. And they are _____to choose liberty and eternal life, through the _____Mediator of all men, or to choose _____and death, according to the captivity and _____of the devil; for he _____that all men might be _____like unto himself.

2 Nephi 2:27

BUT TO BE
LEARNED
IS GOOD IF THEY
HEARKEN
UNTO THE COUNSELS OF
GOD.

2 NEPHI 9:28-29

O that _____ plan of the _____ one! O the _____, and the frailties, and the foolishness of _____! When they are _____ they think they are _____, and they hearken not unto the _____ of God, for they set it aside, supposing they _____ of themselves, wherefore, their _____ is foolishness and it _____ them not. And they shall _____.
But to be learned is _____ if they _____ unto the counsels of _____.

2 Nephi 9:28–29

For we _____diligently to write, to _____our children, and also our brethren, to _____in Christ, and to be reconciled to _____; for we know that it is by _____that we are saved, after ___we can do.

And we _____of Christ, we _____in Christ, we _____of Christ, we _____of Christ, and we _____according to our prophecies, that our _____may know to what _____they may look for a _____of their sins.

2 Nephi 25:23, 26

THERE SHALL BE MANY WHICH SHALL SAY:

EAT
DRINK
AND BE
MERRY

FOR TOMORROW WE DIE: AND IT SHALL BE WELL WITH US...THERE SHALL BE MANY WHICH SHALL TEACH AFTER THIS MANNER, FALSE AND VAIN AND FOOLISH DOCTRINES

2 NEPHI 28:7-9

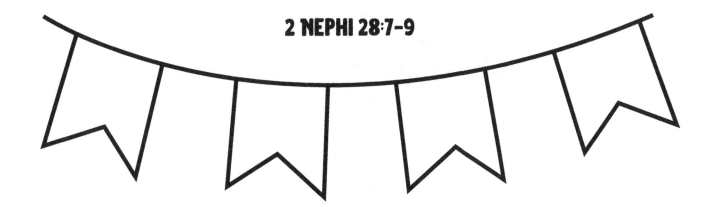

Yea, and there _____be many which shall say: Eat, _____, and be merry, for tomorrow we _____; and it shall be _____with us. And there shall also be _____which shall say: ____, drink, and be merry; nevertheless, _____God—he will justify in committing a _____sin; yea, ____a little, _____the advantage of one because of his words, _____a pit for thy neighbor; there is no _____in this; and do all these _____, for tomorrow we ____; and if it so be that we are _____, God will _____us with a _____stripes, and at last we shall be saved in the _____of God.
Yea, and there shall be _____which shall _____after this manner, false and _____and foolish doctrines, and shall be _____up in their _____, and shall seek _____to hide their counsels from the _____; and their works shall be in the _____.

2 Nephi 28:7–9

And now, my _____brethren, after ye have gotten into this _____and narrow _____, I would _____if all is done? Behold, I say unto you, _____; for ye have ____come thus far _____it were by the word of _____with unshaken _____in him, relying wholly upon the _____of him who is mighty to _____.
Wherefore, ye must _____forward with a steadfastness in _____, having a _____brightness of _____, and a love of _____and of all men. Wherefore, if ye shall _____forward, _____upon the word of _____, and _____to the end, behold, thus saith the _____: Ye shall have eternal _____.

2 Nephi 31:19–20

_____speak by the
power of the
_____Ghost; wherefore,
they speak the _____of
Christ. Wherefore, I said
unto you, _____upon the
words of Christ; for
behold, the _____of
Christ will _____you all
things what ye should
_____.

2 Nephi 32:3

YE MUST *pray always,* AND NOT FAINT

2 NEPHI 32:8-9

And now, my beloved _____, I perceive that ye _____ still in your _____; and it grieveth me that I must _____ concerning this thing. For if ye would _____ unto the _____ which teacheth a man to _____, ye would know that ye must pray; for the evil _____ teacheth not a man to _____, but teacheth him that he must _____ pray.
But behold, I say unto you that ye must _____ always, and not _____; that ye must not _____ any thing unto the _____ save in the first _____ ye shall _____ unto the Father in the name of Christ, that he will _____ thy performance unto thee, that thy _____ may be for the _____ of thy soul.

2 Nephi 32:8–9

when ye are in the

SERVICE

♡♡♡♡♡♡♡♡♡♡♡♡

of your fellow beings ye

are only in the

SERVICE

♡♡♡♡♡♡♡♡♡♡♡♡

of your God.

MOSIAH 2:17

And behold, I _____ you
these things that ye may
learn _____; that ye may
_____ that when ye are
in the _____ of your
fellow _____ ye are only
in the service of your
_____.

Mosiah 2:17

For the natural man is an enemy to God, and has been from the fall of Adam, and will be, forever and ever, unless he yields to the enticings of the Holy Spirit, and putteth off the natural man and becometh a saint through the atonement of Christ the Lord, and becometh as a child, submissive, meek, humble, patient, full of love, willing to submit to all things which the Lord seeth fit to inflict upon him, even as a child doth submit to his father.

Mosiah 3:19

For the _____man is an enemy
to God, and has _____from the
fall of _____, and will be, forever
and ever, unless he _____to the
enticings of the _____Spirit, and
_____off the _____man and
becometh a _____through the
_____of Christ the Lord,
and becometh as a _____,
submissive, _____, humble,
patient, _____of love, willing to
_____to all things which the
Lord seeth ____to inflict
_____him, even as a child doth
submit to his _____.

Mosiah 3:19

But this _____I can tell you, that if ye do not _____yourselves, and your _____, and your words, and _____deeds, and _____the commandments of God, and _____in the faith of what ye have _____concerning the coming of our _____, even unto the _____of your lives, ye must _____. And now, O ____, remember, and _____not.

Mosiah 4:30

And he shall go forth,
suffering pains &
afflictions
& temptations
of every kind;
and this that the word might
be fulfilled which saith
he will take upon him
the pains
& the sicknesses
of his people.

Alma 7:11–13

And he shall go _____, suffering pains and _____and temptations of every _____; and this that the _____might be fulfilled which _____he will take upon ____the pains and the sicknesses of his _____.
And he will ____upon him _____, that he may _____the bands of death which _____his people; and he will _____upon him their _____, that his _____may be filled ____mercy, according to the _____, that he may know _____to the flesh how to _____his people according to _____infirmities.
Now the Spirit _____all things; nevertheless the _____of God suffereth according to the _____that he might take upon him the ____of his people, that he might ____ out their transgressions according to the _____of his deliverance; and now behold, this is the _____which is in me.

Alma 7:11–13

if ye have faith ye hope for things which are not seen, which are true

Alma 32:21

And now as I said concerning _____—faith is not to have a perfect _____ of things; therefore if ye have faith ye hope for _____ which are not seen, which are _____.

Alma 32:21

O, REMEMBER, MY SON, AND LEARN WISDOM IN THY YOUTH; YEA, LEARN IN THY YOUTH TO KEEP THE COMMANDMENTS OF GOD.

ALMA 37:35

O, _____, my son, and _____wisdom in thy youth; yea, learn in thy _____to keep the commandments of

_____.

Alma 37:35

REPENT & FORSAKE YOUR SINS

ALMA 39:9

Now my _____, I would that ye should _____and _____your sins, and go no more after the _____of your ____, but cross yourself in all these things; for _____ye do this ye can in nowise _____the kingdom of God. Oh, _____, and take it upon you, and _____yourself in these things.

Alma 39:9

WICKEDNESS NEVER WAS HAPPINESS

ALMA 41:10

Do not _____, because it has been _____concerning restoration, that ye _____be restored from sin to _____. Behold, I say unto you, wickedness _____was happiness.

Alma 41:10

And now, my sons, remember, remember that it is upon the ROCK of our Redeemer, who is CHRIST, the Son of God, that ye must build your foundation

Helaman 5:12

And now, my _____, remember, remember that it is _____the _____of our Redeemer, who is Christ, the ____of God, that ye must _____your foundation; that when the _____shall send forth his mighty _____, yea, his shafts in the whirlwind, yea, when all his hail and his _____storm shall _____upon you, it shall have no power over you to ____you down to the ____of misery and endless ___, because of the ____upon which ye are ____, which is a ____foundation, a foundation whereon if ____build they cannot ____.

Helaman 5:12

THEREFORE I WOULD THAT YE SHOULD BE PERFECT EVEN AS I, OR YOUR FATHER WHO IS IN HEAVEN IS PERFECT.

3 NEPHI 12:48

Therefore I _____ that ye should be _____ even as I, or your _____ who is in heaven is _____.

3 Nephi 12:48

YE MUST WATCH AND PRAY ALWAYS, LEST YE BE TEMPTED BY THE DEVIL, AND YE BE LED AWAY CAPTIVE BY HIM.

3 NEPHI 18:15, 20-21

Verily, _____, I say unto you, ye must _____and pray _____, lest ye be tempted by the _____, and ye be led _____captive by him. And whatsoever ye shall ____the Father in my _____, which is ____, believing that ye shall _____, behold it shall be given unto you. Pray in your _____unto the Father, _____in my name, that your _____and your children may be _____.

3 Nephi 18:15, 20-21

FAITH IS THINGS WHICH ARE HOPED FOR AND NOT SEEN; WHEREFORE, DISPUTE NOT BECAUSE YE SEE NOT, FOR YE RECEIVE NO WITNESS UNTIL AFTER THE TRIAL OF YOUR FAITH.

Esther 12:6

And now, I, _____, would
speak somewhat
_____these things; I
would show unto the
_____that faith is things
which are _____for and not
seen; wherefore, _____not
because ye ____not, for ye
receive no _____until
after the _____of your
_____.

Esther 12:6

for if they HUMBLE themselves before me, and have FAITH in me, then will I make WEAK things become STRONG unto them.

Esther 12:27

And if _____come unto me I will _____unto them ____ weakness. I give unto ____weakness that ____may be _____; and my _____is sufficient for ____men that _____themselves before ____; for if they humble themselves _____me, and have _____in me, then will I _____weak _____become _____unto them.

Esther 12:27

YE SHALL HAVE HOPE THROUGH THE ATONEMENT OF CHRIST AND THE POWER OF HIS RESURRECTION, TO BE RAISED UNTO LIFE ETERNAL

MORONI 7:41

And _____ is it that ye shall _____ for? Behold I say unto you that ye shall have _____ through the atonement of _____ and the _____ of his resurrection, to be _____ unto life eternal, and this because of your _____ in him according to the _____.

Moroni 7:41

BUT CHARITY IS THE PURE LOVE OF CHRIST, AND IT ENDURETH FOREVER; AND WHOSO IS FOUND POSSESSED OF IT AT THE LAST DAY, IT SHALL BE WELL WITH HIM.

MORONI 7:45, 47-48

And _____suffereth _____, and is kind, and _____not, and is not puffed __, seeketh not her ____, is not easily _____, thinketh no evil, and rejoiceth not in _____but rejoiceth in the _____, beareth all _____, believeth all things, hopeth ____things, endureth all things.
But _____is the pure _____of Christ, and it _____forever; and whoso is _____possessed of it at the last ____, it shall be ____with him. Wherefore, my _____brethren, pray unto the _____with all the energy of _____, that ye may be filled with this _____, which he hath bestowed _____all who are true followers of his ____, Jesus Christ; that ye may become the _____of God; that when he ____appear we shall be ____him, for we shall see him as __is; that we may have this _____; that we may be _____even as he is _____. Amen.

Moroni 7:45, 47–48

ASK GOD, THE ETERNAL FATHER, IN THE NAME OF CHRIST, IF THESE THINGS ARE NOT TRUE; AND IF YE SHALL ASK WITH A SINCERE HEART, WITH REAL INTENT, HAVING FAITH IN CHRIST, HE WILL MANIFEST THE TRUTH OF IT UNTO YOU, BY THE POWER OF THE HOLY GHOST

MORONI 10:4-5

And when ye shall _____these things, I would exhort ____that ye would _____God, the Eternal Father, in the _____of Christ, if these things are not _____; and if ye shall ____with a sincere heart, with _____intent, having _____in Christ, he will manifest the _____of it unto ____, by the power of the ____Ghost. And by the _____of the Holy Ghost ye may _____the truth of all _____.

Moroni 10:4–5

IF YOU ENJOYED THIS BOOK, PLEASE LEAVE A REVIEW.

FOLLOW US ONLINE!

@LATTER.DAY.DESIGNS

LATTER-DAY DESIGNS

Made in the USA
Las Vegas, NV
01 March 2024

86342091R00031